Tortoise

Remember Me Series

By

Caroline Norsk

Caroline Norsk

Copyright © 2014 by Caroline Norsk

All rights reserved. No part of this book may be used or reproduced in any manner whatsoever without the express written permission of the publisher except for the use of brief quotations in a book review

Image Credits: Royalty free images reproduced under license from various stock image repositories. Under a creative commons licenses.

Remember me I am a tortoise.

Remember me I am also a turtle, but an ordinary turtle isn't a tortoise.

Remember me I am a land turtle.

Remember me I have a carapace, which is my house.

Remember me I can't swim.

Remember me I usually eat plants.

Remember me I have stubby, elephant-like feet, unlike the flippers of ordinary turtles.

Remember me I have a heavier domed shell than ordinary turtles.

Tortoise

Remember me I love to be alone all my life.

Remember me I don't care for my young after they hatch.

Tortoise

Remember me if you see anything like me, such as your friend's sunglasses, say it's "testudinal."

Remember me you won't be able to tell my sex until I reach a certain size.

Remember me the scales of my shells are of the same material as your fingernails.

Remember me if I have a light-colored shell, I hail from a hot place.

Tortoise

Remember me although I can't swim, I can hold my breath for a long time.

Remember me my shell parts are all bones and I also have bones inside of me.

Remember me when I'm startled, I hide inside my shell.

Caroline Norsk

Remember me my shell is sensitive to touch.

Tortoise

Remember me I can be your pet.

Remember me I have a keen sense of smell.

Tortoise

Thank you.

Good Luck.

Made in the USA
San Bernardino, CA
25 November 2017